FORGET THE

BUSINESS PLAN USE THIS SHORT MODEL

Tiisetso Maloma

PUBLISHING AND COPYRIGHT

FORGET THE BUSINESS PLAN USE THIS SHORT MODEL

By Tiisetso Maloma

Print ISBN: 978-1481812696

eBook ISBN: 978-1-300-68920-1

www.tiisetsomaloma.com

Published by Maloma Publishing

Editing by Mmatshepo Chiloane

Layout, eBook conversion and distribution by www.bulabuka.co.za

SOCIAL MEDIA

SUBSCRIBE TO BLOG *www.tiisetsomaloma.com*

TWITTER - @tiisetsomaloma

FACEBOOK.COM/tiisetsomaloma

QUORA – tiisetsomaloma

INSTAGRAM – tiisetsomaloma

CONTENTS

THE AUTHOR, TIISETSO MALOMA

Tiisetso is a writer and entrepreneur. He is the author of The Anxious Entrepreneur, Forget The business Plan Use This Short Model, Township Biz Fastrack, and creator of the EBC Business Model.

Maloma went to the University of Johannesburg and completed a Diploma in Accounting and a Post Graduate Diploma in Forensic Auditing.

Tiisetso founded STARTUP PICNIC, Gabble Heights Clothing (closed), Bula Buka, Maloma Publishing and Practice DVD among other startups.

- -

Tiisetso successfully founded/started and project managed several startups with no resources. His skill is picking resources to deliberately do without and minimum viability essentials to gain traction with.

With zero budgets, he led a few successful marketing campaigns.

Tiisetso has published articles and featured in various media platforms: Under30CEO, Power FM, NSBC, How We Made It in Africa, Business Report, Destiny Man, Cliffcentral, Radio 2000 FM, YFM, Alex FM, Hashtag Radio and many more.

His repertoire of entities he has served includes Nedbank, SABC, ACM Gold, The Hope Factory, CSIR, Soul City, Moshito and Meerkat Media.

ABOUT THE BOOK

Like most people, I started my entrepreneurship journey being a business plan disciple and also used it as a tool to learn business – because the world's conventions recommended only it.

Halfway through I realized a business plan doesn't teach and it isn't a swift planning tool. It is tedious to manage, does not help diagnose weak areas and is not agile to ever changing environments and circumstances.

I then built a model which readily reminded me of essential business components to concentrate on; it is diagnostic, responsive and agile.

After reading this book, by referring to single page canvas of this model, you will be able to swiftly start, plan or brainstorm your entrepreneurship project.

This book is about an entrepreneurship management tool or business model called EBC Business Model Canvas. EBC stands for Essential Business Components. Download the one page canvas for free here www.tiisetsomaloma.com.

This book is makes entrepreneurship uncomplicated, efficient to understand and manage.

The book thoroughly explains 6 interdependent essential business components of this model: 4 core technical components and 2 that deal with the entrepreneur's attitude, health, decision making swiftness and persistence.

It's makes things easier for entrepreneurs by keeping the main things main.

EBC Business Model is useable in all industries, on service or tangible products.

INTRODUCTION ~ FORGET THE BUSINESS PLAN, USE THIS SHORT MODEL

Don't you just dislike the long business plan format? In all my entrepreneurial endeavors I've found that the most important component is not the business plan but the entrepreneur, the product and the consumers. Think product, not business plan. Product not business plan! Some call this "the business model".

As an entrepreneur you are the star of the show. What's important is your ability to innovate your product, in order to get a kick out of your customers. It's your ability to navigate yourself in solidifying your business model. All this is a process of self discovery and learning.

A business plan is a set of items/topics that economists reckon are important in determining the feasibility of a business. No lie, those topics are important, but more so to economists than to you. As an entrepreneur you have to see them with different eyes, entrepreneurial eyes.

Entrepreneurs are not seasonal. Entrepreneurs are about creating profiting opportunities, given good or bad circumstances. When economic conditions are good in a particular year, it means entrepreneurs have done a good job the previous year; such delayed information is brought to you courtesy of economists.

There are economists and there are entrepreneurs. These are 2 different spheres of performance. To be an entrepreneur one requires entrepreneurial thinking, not that an economist cannot venture entrepreneurially. Entrepreneurship is about realizing opportunity or creating opportunity and of course trying hard to profit from it.

On the other hand, economists present information, assessing and predicting risks and opportunities. Entrepreneurs harness risks, they peer forward with innovation and swim through the risks in order to profit.

For me innovation is about simplicity and efficiency. The normal business plan format is too long and tedious. Unless you require a loan from a bank, you do not need to prepare it, if you do, hire someone to do it for you, of course with your guidance. Use the short format I have prepared below. I call it <u>essential business components (EBC)</u>.

Without too much sensation as to why I hate the conventional business plan format, here is what I have devised.

THE MODEL - ESSENTIAL BUSINESS COMPONENTS (EBC)

Please note: a product in this book refers to any business solution/offering, either a physical product, soft product or a service.

It all starts with an idea to create a product or start a business service; then making the product. The second stage is selling that product (sales and marketing). This is where most businesses have it hard. It is a very important and crucial stage; a stage at which you have an opportunity to connect your product with society. It's an actual and opportune stage to reflect on whether your product entices sales.

Here are the essential components to your business's success. Forget the business-plan, use this short format or model.

The business model below applies to all sorts of business types: music business, IT-start-ups, clothing, consulting, services etc.

1. ABSOLUTE PRODUCT

It all starts with an idea to create a product; then making the product.

Below are characteristics which your product or brand has to have if it is to be profitable. They are elaborative. Apply them to your product.

It has to serve an identifiable purpose(s) or deliver value to consumers

Consumers buy products for absolute purposes that the products will serve. Be it even that the product brings joy to them, or tickles their fancy. The point being, the product brings a certain satisfaction or use to them. And the satisfaction or use is brought about by acquiring your product.

It has to be of better value from your competition, in the eye of consumers

It could be the price, feature or design difference. A cheaper product may be the reason for consumers to buy your product and not the competition's.

There are many reasons which could make consumers choose your product over your competitor's. Always chase that reason and imbed it in your product.

Appeal to a need or want. It could be an old need/want, or a new need/want that which you created yourself

A new need is a need that consumers weren't absolutely aware that they had, but because of your product they now realise that need, and your product becomes the solution.

Your product has to add a difference to people's lives. Consumers must be willing to pay money to have that difference.

Deliver efficiency

Your clientele has to be better off with your product. They must be glad they possess your product. It should make a better difference in their lives somehow.

Easily defined products and product features

It's about describing what your product can do for consumers. When products/services are easily described and their use is easily understood, they become easier to sell. It also becomes easier for you to relate what the product will do for the consumer, and easier for consumers to understand what the product will do for them.

This helps consumers readily identify what your product will do for them.

It is also a quick way to close a sale. This is your product's hook.

Good quality, good after sales service and maintenance

This is how you protect your product's use, in that it's always in use and serving its purpose. This is also how you maximise the value of your business brand, which then makes your brand the trusted among plenty.

Well branded product

Branding is the layer that covers your product or a layer which stands for your product.

You need a logo. A logo is a sharp and distinctive mark which says "I made this product, this product of such stature".

Your product's packaging is crucial; it should communicate a psychology that captures consumers. It should also explicitly communicate your business's name. When people think of a good product, your brand should come up.

Don't take forever building your product

We all are in chase of perfection, to better our products. Do not take forever perfecting your product. Things change, people change, relevance changes; who knows; someone might come up with an idea similar to yours.

Don't overload your product, the best way to test its viability is to release it in the market, and improve it along the way.

For as long as a product is able to serve a particular purpose and add value in the market, people will be willing to pay money for it.

The best way to learn as an entrepreneur (value provider) is through engaging your product with the market (selling), as soon as possible. Whatever the stage of the product, it must serve value or purpose that which people can exchange money for.

Say you take time loading features onto your product, and then release the product into the market, the market will give you feedback on what to tweak.

It would take more time to tweak and return the product to the market than if you had less features. Another reason not to overload your product is, once you get into the market and competition strikes, the extra unloaded features can be used as ammunition to stay ahead.

I want to quote something that Rick Alden (founder of Skull Candy) once said. I struggled to find the precise quote, paraphrasing will do. He said, the first one to get to the market, is the market leader. I think he was pointing to what I stressed above. Skull Candy didn't take that long to get to the market. And as they were in the market, they learned a lot of things which helped the company become stronger. This would have probably not been the case had they delayed to launch. Skull Candy is a headphone leader in the outdoor action sports market.

With Gabble Heights Clothing, we started off with one t-shirt range (the gabble sign fraternity), of course we wanted to have other clothing items, but our budget didn't allow. So this gave us an opportunity to market one range, which was easier than if we had multiple items. Through our interaction with the market, we learned a lot and with the money made thus far, we introduced other items.

Protect product use value through innovation and consistent enhancement

The truth of the matter is, everything changes, people change, competition gets tougher, and other factors like piracy take course. Say you release your product this year and people buy it, then next year and the following years, they have no reason to buy it again because they have it already. Your duty is to then give them such a reason to continue buying. The role of a business is to make money everyday (or year) if possible and keep making it. So, the year following the product release, release something that the same consumer who bought the first product can buy, so as to keep making money.

Even if it's an enhancement of the current product, those that bought old one would want the new one because it has something that the old doesn't have. In this way you will continue making money.

But be very careful not to totally take the crap out of the previous product. You might upset your first consumers (I'm not totally sure of this, think it through).

Take apple for instance, it's always taking money out of people' pockets, it's always making money, as businesses should, and as they are meant to. From iPhone 1, you want iPhone 4s and now iPhone 5. So they are living up to business philosophy, "ever making money".

- - - -

Another example is Google. Since its inception, it's been improving its main product which is the search engine. Again it has been acquiring other properties that now make money for it; Youtube, Adsense (former Oingo), Android, etc. If their search engine business was to become less profitable, it has invested its profits in other revenue driving streams/products. The amazing part about Google is that they also buy companies that add extra service on their search engine business, which is their founding product.

- - - - -

I'm not dictating to you how your product should be. I'm sure there are many other ways to think of this process. Take what you think will work for you. Please do share of how you do it, here tiisetsomalomablog@gmail.com.

2. MARKETING

This is an opportunity to appeal to society. It's a chance to relate your product offerings to a need/want that your product meets.

Do not underestimate consumers; they are intelligent; quality, innovation, respect, value, societal value and creativity appeals to them.

With the following sub subheadings, I relate concepts which you can use to attract customers.

Marking your targets

Don't you just hate it when smart people ask you who your target market is? I deliberately used "marking your targets" as the sub heading to component number 2 (marketing), instead of "target market". I don't want to sound like those smart guys that always have difficult questions for us less smart entrepreneurs. Think "marking targets", not "target market". The idea is to sell quickest to those likely to buy quick.

Alright; you are an entrepreneur, you are thinking to either make money from selling your product or you want to make a living out of something you are passionate about.

Product ideas come to us in many different ways. It might be that you weren't thinking of a target market when creating the product, all you wanted was to create a product which you believe will be of value to people. Or maybe you were overwhelmed with an idea, or inspiration, to create that company, brand, or product.

Whatever your reasons for creating that company/brand/product, after having carefully considered and installed what is emphasised above (1. absolute product), you will need a mechanism for attracting sales to that product.

A probability is that, as a small business or start-up, you do not have a marketing budget, and even if you have a sizeable budget, you don't know for sure if that budget and your marketing plan will yield justifiable sales. Or maybe you have no clue how to market your product.

Here is how you start, identify who is likely to buy your product. How would you get hold of such persons to relate your product to? There you go, you have a target market or target markets (that's after you have identified them). This is a stage that learnered marketers and economists would call "relating product-value-proposition to audience".

Now you know who you want to sell to, and now it's time to get a hold of them.

- - - - -

Below I list possible ways to reach your target market

(a) Direct sales pitches

Direct sales pitching is when you approach people (the targets you have marked per above) directly, individually or in their groups. It could be at their work place or a gathering of some sort, wherever or however you deem appropriate. If it's at a gathering, you may have to pay to reach them. It could be by renting an exhibition stand or something.

As a small business, you know what you can afford and what you can't. The best thing to do would be to use mediums you can afford.

(b) Reaching your audience through advertising

Another method is by buying advertising space in a newspaper, magazine, on Facebook, placing a radio ad or any other means of advertising.

The rationale should be whether your likely clientele makes use of the medium which you want to advertise on.

It's up to you as the entrepreneur to determine whether you can afford such advertising rates, and/or whether you can sustain them. Decide whether such spending justifies your sales forecast.

(c) Penetrative marketing

As explained above, you could start off by marketing targets of people you could or want to sell to.

After identifying who is likely to buy your product, you can start grouping them according to different genres; for example: commerce, IT, hip hop, etc. There are also many ways you can group people within a society; such as through their careers, language, lifestyle, etc.

After categorising the kind of people you could sell to; figure out the following:

How to get hold of each group?

Which group is likely to buy the product?

Which group should I assign a higher priority to?

Which group isn't likely to buy my product?

Which group is inexpensively reachable?

Are any of the groups sensitive to how they are approached and/or spoken to?

How am I going to penetrate each group?

Which group will contribute most sales?

In what way should I relate my product so that I get their full attention and pockets?

How do I conscientise each group towards what I am selling?

You the entrepreneur should figure out the above. It's your money and you have to decide on how best to spend it. The idea is that for every cent you going to spent on marketing, it should yield sales.

In other words, your marketing campaigns should be able to penetrate or conscientise each group identified, and generate sales.

(d) PR – pubic relations

Whenever we think PR, we think of paying an agency. If you don't have the budget for PR, you can do it yourself. Google the essentials for a press release.

Even Mark Cuban says start-ups don't need a PR agency. Money is too tight. I even heard James Altucher alluding to Mark Cuban's sentiments.

PR is a process where you relate to the media about your magnificent product, in the hope that they will feature it, and therefore you can get exposure to their audience. And it's free.

> *Here is a story of successful self PR. Ron Henry, a photographer, decided to take matters into his hands and*

make comfortable camera straps that position cameras readily for quick shots.

He borrowed $5000 from a friend to make the belts, build a website for taking orders and bought a banner ad on an online wedding forum.

There wasn't any marketing budget, so he approached photography bloggers/blogs, related his product and gave them freebie samples. A major and boosting part of his sales came from people that saw/read a review from the bloggers. The company is called Black Rapid; it makes over $6 million annually. Here is the story's link http://www.inc.com/april-joyner/bootstrap-how-black-rapid-won-over-bloggers.html

Now they have added other camera accessories to their product line-up.

You, the entrepreneur can create a database of industry related blogs or mediums; then send them your press release and/or with a sample (if you can afford, prioritise people if you have to). Collecting a database can be a lot of work; you can do 3 a week.

PR advice from an expert

There is a great community of South African entrepreneurs on twitter, under the hash tag #buildSA #advancingSA. On Thursdays we have experts come dissect certain topics to us. The other day we had Shonisani Makhari, CEO of PR firm http://flowsa.co.za, schooling us on PR. Below are the points he highlighted. If you are going to do your own PR, these are crucial. If you don't have money for PR, you can do it yourself.

- PR is a third party endorsement; indirectly or directly i.e.

  celebrities, media, etc.

- Create stories that capture the media's attention. Will your story sell their papers?

- When a journalist writes a story about your product/business, it carries credibility.

- News is created based on timing, content and source.

- Know which journalists write about your industry.

- Construct an article that's news worthy, create contact and push your story.

- People get PR wrong because their story is all about them but nothing of interest to media's audience.

- Media loves stats.

- Mention what problems can be uniquely be solved by your product.

- You will go quicker with hired help, but think costs. Can you afford?

- Don't lie, media always finds out.

- Don't say anything off record, ever.

I take it bootstrapping excludes hiring a PR firm. With every cent you might spend on marketing, always figure out how much value that spent will return to you in sales.

Safe marketing

A brand like Gucci, for example, advertises in magazines such as GQ because the kind of clientele that read GQ either: wear Gucci, can afford clothing at Gucci's price range, or aspire to wear Gucci.

I call this safe marketing. Not because it's less edgy, nor is it because I'm less risky. No, I'm very risky and I like this concept of safe marketing. My duty as an entrepreneur is to have a good (absolute) product and realise sales quick. This concept I call safe marketing. It's a way to rationalise the people who you advertise to, based on their likelihood of buying your product the quickest. Cash flow is king, it's vital for your business's success, you need it ASAP. Therefore you need to realise it ASAP.

With your little marketing budget, rather use it to market to a market that is likely to buy the earliest, so you keep your cash inflow from sales going, as quickly as possible. From there on you can branch into other markets since you will have a cash injecting customer-base and a spare budget. Your drive is to realise sales ASAP.

With your small marketing budget, rather use it to advertise to a market that is likely to buy your product the earliest, this way you can have cash inflow from sales, as quickly as possible. You can then venture into other markets given that you will have cash injecting customer-base and a spare budget. Your drive should be to realise sales ASAP.

You should use marketing platforms or methods that you believe will bring sales the quickest, especially if you do not have a big budget.

For start-ups, marketing to a group of people that you are certain will buy your product/service, is better than marketing to a group you aren't confident will buy from you.

At least 2 marketing concepts

"Conservative guys buy core products, core guys don't buy conservative". This was said by Rick Alden, founder of Skull Candy. Think of this quote until it registers. This is a powerful quote. The thing about core groups or subcultures in society is that they are core. They are true to what they like. If they like something, they like it, if they don't then they don't.

As I said before, most entrepreneurs start out without having a clear target market, if any at all. That's ok. We just want to sell to people, any people.

My advice is, which I'm using on my current projects, your marketing has to have at least two concepts or strategies, one for the core market and the other for non-core groups. It's clear that the core concept will work on both the core guys and the non core guys, as even folks in suits aspire to be core at something or actually are core at something. But the non core (conservative) concept will work on everyone outside the core group. So at least you will be safe, reaching more people, in a well thought out method.

If you would like, you can have multiple campaigns, each for a different group. But you need to always consider your budget. It's also about maximising every cent of your budget. The trick, as mentioned already, is to get sales as soon as possible. Then only later, when your budget allows, can you do other marketing tricks, but by then you would have learned how to maximise your Rand spent.

Dramatisation and spunk

On absolute product above, I mentioned easy description of your product. Once you have the description on easy, its time to hook the sales.

Given your product has the characteristics of an absolute product; it therefore means it has a hook. The sales part is where you hook your prospect.

If your advertising is dull, it might distract informing people of what it is you are selling or offering.

The spunk is what draws people's attention to the advertisement. When you are dramatic in explaining your product offerings, it's easier to attract people's attention to what you are selling.

The big question should be, 'How do I conscientise a certain market to my product?' 'How do you speak to them?' and 'Where do I speak to them?'

Thereafter can you start thinking spunk and dramatisation.

Social media

Being on social media doesn't guarantee your product will get traction. Not everyone likes everything. The truth is that your friends on Facebook don't have the same tastes.

But those who do like your product will probably like your Facebook page or follow your twitter account. Also, your friends who don't necessarily like your product will share it out of friendship. Then maybe their friends, who might like the product, will share it with their friends, and so on.

Social media is good. However, it should not be the only tool you use for attracting customers. There should always be something bigger than social media that you are doing.

With Gabble Heights Clothing, we learned the hard way with using social media as the main marketing method (I'm not referring to pay ads). It worked for some time, as we had a good product but lost traction along the way as nothing outside social media was happening. So, in effect, we had no content to share on social media. I mean content on ways gabble heights was connecting with the outside world besides on the internet.

Doing big things elsewhere (e.g. social marketing elsewhere), means you will have exciting content to share, therefore increasing your traction and following on social media.

I think social media works well when its consumers informing people of your brand. Then you being on social media would be to grab the attention and share it.

Communicate your innovation.

** On the bonus articles, I have added 2 articles on social media.

Selling aspiration

We all aspire to look a certain way. This aspiration is brought about by different things e.g. magazines, film, friends, celebrities, books, etc.

Make people aspire to own your product. Sync your product with something or someone 'kool'. You could use methods such as a photo-shoots, events, music, celebrity ambassadorship, painting, or whatever other way.

The sync should have people buy into your product.

The determining task now is to distribute (market) that aspiration representation.

Sales vs. advertising

As I said, marketing is an opportunity to relate your product to society. Advertising is a form of marketing where you display or entice your prospect to your product.

You can say advertising is an attractive or dramatic mechanic of attracting your prospect's attention.

So sales and advertising are forms of marketing. An advert can have a sales pitch, wherein it describes product advantages and features. But I don't think it's enough that an advert pitches product features and advantages. There has to be something about it that draws people's attention to it.

Imagine a newspaper, magazine or television has many other product adverts; what will steal people's attention to yours.

I'm not too sure of people buying a product because of the goodness of the advert; maybe they do maybe they don't. But, the function of marketing is to attract attention to a product and inspire sales. It's another issue if that product doesn't meet the potential customer's expectations. Your job as an entrepreneur is to make sure your product meets those expectations.

3. CASH FLOW

To make a product normally requires some financial investment. Whether it is to buy material or pay someone to help make the product.

The pinnacle of it all is financial management. Cash is king. You make, sell and remake. There has to be a profit. There has to be re-investment. This is how growth takes shape.

Cash flow management is one area I learned the hard way, I had overlooked my sustenance. Even entrepreneurs have to eat, drink (which can be sacrificed) and be roofed.

Rationalise every cent spent. Sort out the budget for production, recurring production, marketing, distribution, etc. You must get a sense of what your expenditure on marketing will generate in terms of sales.

Even if you are bootstrapping, it's vital that you know your finances. Keep a separate personal bank account to the business. The way in which you record the money doesn't matter, as long as you can understand it, know how much you have and the information can easily be translated into financial statements.

Remember that keeping your receipts will get you deductions when the tax man calls, as he always does.

Reducing expenses

The notion that proper planning saves you money applies even in business. Most times, us start-up entrepreneurs prefer prepaid services and goods as we cannot afford to attach ourselves onto contracts, which most times offer discounted rates. That is good entrepreneur acumen.

For instance you could save on website hosting if you paid yearly instead of monthly or save more by paying for 3 years in advance. But this all depends on how your cash flow looks.

Timing in most processes is crucial in determining the price value of purchases. During Gabble Heights Clothing, we were almost always chasing close deadlines. Had we planned properly, we would have probably saved on costs of collecting materials from suppliers, as most of them delivered, but had their own delivery schedule which, most of the times, we couldn't wait for as our deadlines were too close.

From time to time, look at your income statement, or as you might call it "expenditure sheet". Look at what is really necessary, and what expenses can be reduced (by paying yearly for example). Closely analyse the expenses and delivery of items, as some may be clustered and then discounted.

Importantly, before effecting costs, analyse how each affects the business wholly, both now and later. Your priority should be protecting your brand's value and profits.

4. DISTRIBUTION

Ok, so your product is now good and you are confident of the marketing plan. The next stage is the distribution. Distribution is a process of handing over products to consumers, or a point where consumers can inspect your products, a point where sales are realised. As we know, without sales profits can't be realised.

In a service business, distribution is the point of executing the service.

How are you going to get products to your clients?

How are they going to get the products from you and how are you going to get the products to them? This process has to be efficient both for you and them.

Distribution is the manner in which consumers will access your product and consume it; depending on your kind of business, be it you sell online, through your shop, or through someone's shop (e.g. retailer). Either consumer gets your product directly from you or an external retailer or distributor.

- - - - -

For the purposes of explaining this component, distributors and retailers are one and the same.

Dealing with distributors

I know for a new business, it might be hard to get distributers or retailers on your side.

A good absolute product and a good marketing plan (the ones above) are necessary to win a distributor or retailer over.

If a product's uses are easily identified, it becomes easy for a distributor to get a feel of whether people will buy that product or not. The marketing strategy's duty is to convince the distributor/retailer that people will specifically buy your product from them.

Highlight how your product will work for their store, as in who will buy it. Figure out ways of making your product work in that particular store. What in-store advertising or campaigning methods you can use. What is allowed and what isn't allowed.

An important matter is provision of product training. Train the distributors on your product and always check if they are ok with the training. Continued training and engagement with distributors is an opportunity to learn of your product's performance. It's an opportunity to learn what information consumers revert to the distributor. It's an opportunity for the distributor to give their opinion on areas you can improve and other competitive products that are in-store.

When distributors say no to you

If retailers/distributors say no to you, ask for their reasons for declining. Ask yourself if the feedback requires you to change/tweak your product. I know for most entrepreneurs, it's about breaking conventions. Now and then, assess your product's usability.

There have been instances where my products didn't fit a prospective retailer's product focus. They have said no, I got upset. But later I realised its ok, I don't have to tweak my product just because it's different. I remember I twice approached YDE (Young Designers

Emporium) with Gabble Heights Clothing. The second time, the lady I was dealing with was nice to explain why they wouldn't consider my product. One was that my clothes weren't trend based (their prerequisite); two was that our style wasn't what they looked for. And it wasn't that my product was bad, it's just that it didn't fit their product focus or style. They have a business model and we didn't fit into their model.

We had a choice; to either tweak our product so to suit their business model, or pursue our style and find other ways to distribute. Well let's say we are working on a store of our own.

We had a choice of adjusting our product in order to suit YDE, but we chose not to. We devised other means of how we could get our product to consumers. It's taking longer, but we are fine with that. We could have adjusted our product and would have maybe gotten in, it wouldn't have been bad, but we chose not to. If you asked me why, I would say that we are about bringing our product as we want it to be, not as distributors want. It's a decision we took and there isn't any regret. We figured that we started the business to create products our way, but also (people love innovation) in a way that people would like, and thus far people love our style.

Another option was to tweak our product to suit the retailer's business model and then get into business, make money, then change things around as our brand would by then command respect amongst retailers, etc. But it's not for us in the instance of gabble heights Clothing.

- - - - -

Starting a revolution in distribution

It's not the end of the world if distributors/retailers say no to your product. What's important is whether the consumer is willing to buy it. It's ok if distributors say no because they have a business model that they need respect as it works for them.

The most important relationship in business is between the product and the end consumer. If distributors don't get your product, reassess if consumers get it. If consumers do get it and distributors don't get it, relate this to the distributors, if there is still no luck with the distributors, its time for a revolution. The revolution means coming up with an innovative distribution plan. Let the distributors know that you are going ahead without them, because consumers get your product.

The question now becomes 'how do I get this product to consumers, of course without conventional distributors, in the most efficient and non-tedious manner?'

I got into the t-shirt business back in 2009, selling "Im a Kool Kid" t-shirts, owned by Antonio Skele. My partner then, Mohlomi Matlala and I were responsible for sales & distribution in Pretoria. The deliberate vision was not to sell through stands, as we thought kool don't do stands at some flea market (and we still do think that). So our sales were person-to-person, and soliciting shops around Pretoria. First of all the t-shirts are that attractive, people want to be attractive, and selling wasn't on some hawker tip. We did well; a R2000 was easy on any Friday night.

When I started selling Gabble Heights in 2010, the strategy was simple, to start from the streets and start approaching shops. We did that. I introduced the brand to a hip hop boutique in Melville called 'Munks Concept Store'. They loved the brand, so they took it in on consignment'. The good street sales and Munks Concept Store taking in the product meant we had an absolute product.

The challenge came when the store wasn't selling any t-shirts. I sat down with Dylan (Munks owner), and he advised me to check my pricing strategy and marketing. He was right. The price was unattractive (@R350) for a clothing brand at our stage and our marketing wasn't penetrative.

I'm not trying to give you a rule of thumb on pricing. I don't have it. I can only give you my opinion based on experiences. What we should have done was let people know the t-shirts are valued at R350 but run an introductory discount sale, say at about 50% less.

The brand's traction would have let us know when to change to R350. If we still got burned at R350, we would have introduced another price strategy.

Do not underestimate the value of easy product description.

Marketing within distribution

The other day I was speaking to my uncle about marketing. He works for South Africa's second biggest liquor marketers (in terms of sales), after the famous South African Brewers.

What he was saying was that distribution is very important to them. It also serves as a marketing function. Media marketing, for them, takes a lesser priority to marketing within distribution. Since they are South Africa's second biggest liquor marketers, distributors value whatever product they bring to the market. In this sense, they market directly to the usual suspects. So I guess marketing at distributor level works wonders for them.

I will explain what he told me in my understanding.

What is important to them is for their brand to occupy shelves and be very visible. There are many ways of making sure your product is visible in-store. I see people using balloons, flashing displayers, posters, etc. The psychology is that consumers should be aware of the product and its possible use.

The psychology to drive is, consumers need your product more than the competition's, within the store.

Running your own distribution

This is when you got your own store, online or physical. First of all, you must believe in your product; that people will buy it.

This is a good model in that you are selling directly to your customers. Again it's scary in that more of your money is on the line; not only money in producing the product but also building/renting/merchandising the store.

I will not say a lot on this form of distribution. But I advise that you learn all that you can on operating a store. Most importantly, use your mind and think of the psychologies that can apply in attracting customers to the store and closing sales.

Psychologies that will be important could be…

Store location.

Window display.

Merchandising.

Service, sales assistant training and product training.

Atmosphere of the store (includes also the above points).

Price vs. value in product.

Purpose of product.

All the best with distributing your product!

Distribution of your product has to happen. This is how you hand your product to consumers. The easier it is for customers to get a hold of your product, the better for you and them, and the easier sales become.

This is where you must deliver efficiently. Keep the customer happy as   possible.

5. RELENTLESSNESS

When all else fails, you have to be prepared to try again. Through failure you learn and come out more experienced and stronger, in other words, you have the opportunity to improve on the above components. You can sharpen all other areas and improve on those areas where you previously lacked. That's how products get better and sales elevate.

6. HAPPINESS (AND HONESTY)

This component was initially not supposed to be included.

But I think happiness in business is important and crucial, in fact it's detrimental. Entrepreneurs are normally passionate people; they get into business to satisfy a need in them to be entrepreneurs, a need which yields them happiness. Even before we reach profiting success, but by merely deciding on being entrepreneurs, we are happy.

Happiness favours a decisive mind

Happiness is best achieved by decisions and actions. Deciding to be an entrepreneur yields satisfaction, that satisfaction brings about joy, which is happiness.

From this point, we can tell that we are happy when we make decisions that put us in a position which serves us with fulfilment, a point where we try to attain progress.

Thus, by having a mind that is always ready to decide to do things that bring us satisfaction and joy, we welcome happiness and we are happy.

So in saying, we can have happiness at any time, just by deciding to do things that bring us fulfilment.

As we can have happiness at any time, just by deciding, it means happiness favours anyone with a decisive attitude. So, happiness is within us. We just have to take decisions to do things that bring us fulfilment, which in turn give us satisfaction, then happiness.

Honesty and foolishness

Most of us entrepreneurs want to be millionaires. But we are very aware that it can't be achieved at the snap of a finger.

It therefore means that we are aware of the need not to be foolish and dishonest with ourselves.

The logical thing to do is to think of schemes that could get us to millions. I'm not talking of unlawful schemes. It could be a business idea. So we are aware that we have to do something of value that will amount to millions when marketed well.

Our logic now tells us to take decisions and take action, e.g. finding a business idea, productising the idea, marketing the idea, etc.

After each action we take, happiness will be upon us. Even when we fail, we know that we have to make a decision to take another action to get us to fulfilment. Happiness is a progressive wheel, which might find humps along the way. It might change direction, but we have to keep getting it into the right direction, by taking decisions. That's how we become happy.

Procrastination

As I was writing this book, I procrastinated a lot. That brought displeasure, anxiety and pain. I knew that the only way to feel joy was when the book is finished. The only way the book would be finished was by writing. So every time, I had to keep deciding to write the book, by taking action.

Happiness is brought about by chasing efficiency

As we established that happiness is brought about by decisions and actions. In taking these decisions and actions, we are hoping to achieve something that will give us fulfilment. We are tying to build something. If we build something that is sustainable, it will give us sustained fulfilment. If you buy a house, that house will give you joy, and since a house is fixed, your joy as well will be fixed.

We are well aware that not everything will go our way, like when trying to buy a house, mishaps can happen, deferring the goal. But you keep trying.

If you set a goal, you will be happy when the goal is achieved. The main parts are, you decided to realise a goal, and then you decided to achieve that goal in a particular way. It might be that you made certain decisions to do things in a certain way, in order to achieve the goal and some of the actions you took might have not worked out. But you keep trying with different approaches.

The heartening point is that you were trying to achieve a goal; you tried to be efficient in achieving that goal so that it could be achieved. Now after failure, you are more efficient as you know what worked and what didn't, and now you are efficient in achieving that particular goal.

So, efficiency is achieved in trying to achieve goals. Without intending to be efficient maybe, you landed at efficiency. Don't despair when you fail, you are just trying to be efficient, take joy in knowing that you are trying to be efficient, welcome failure and mishaps.

A prerequisite of happiness is that we TRY to be efficient in doing things we decided upon. If we don't try to be efficient, we are then dishonest with ourselves and that will yield unhappiness.

Knowingly being inefficient in doing something means you are sabotaging yourself, which could highlight that you weren't willingly happy with the decision to do that particular thing. You weren't prepared to achieve fulfilment and happiness.

Being efficient is doing things the best way you can, through trying.

Say you want to be healthy. There are things that you must decide on. You already know that you can't be healthy if you do not eat healthy and exercise. So you would have to do things that will make you healthy, such as exercising and eating healthy.

The decisions you take to be healthy, require you to be efficient in getting to better health.

Entrepreneurs need good health so they could be efficient.

N.B blessings

Recognise what you value, that which you are grateful for having in your life. Be grateful for every single thing that you value. Let's pursue valuable endeavours. Let's try to create and achieve value. We will feel proud and happy, which in turn is encouragement to create further value.

Extending progress into other people's lives

We should accept that we are not perfect. We know of others' shortcomings, and we also have shortcomings, though sometimes others' shortcomings anger us greatly as if we are perfect.

When you hire an intern, you hire them on the basis that you will offer them perspective on how they can offer you value, in turn they are building value for themselves which then they will use to further their careers. That I'm sure this would bring you happiness.

Be of value to people, it will bring you joy, but if they piss in your face, forgive them anyway. Your joy is in bringing value not destruction. Who wants to mess with a man who brings value into many people's lives? A man who brings value into people's lives invites prosperity.

As a start-up, you can't afford to have inefficient employees. Can you help them be more efficient? Maybe show them the value they need to bring forth in order to have a remunerable bearing in your firm. I've been an employee before, I have been lazy and inefficient, but was given other chances. I bless those who gave me other chances.

Then there are those employees that gossip and are negative, they bring unhappiness and create a negative atmosphere. I don't like those, firing them is possibly the only solution. Such a disease is dangerous, and maybe incurable.

Alright, happiness in business! You are happy when you help people. After they mess up, you will be unhappy when a decision to give them a second chance affects your business's integrity (including profitability).

Over and above all, your decisions should bring happiness, progress and efficiency in your business. Among most, happiness and prosperity is brought about by helping others to prosper. Let's build a prosperous world.

Fence thc negative

You can't thrive when negative energy is around you. You need to cut it off. But negative energy needs to be very aware that you will go ahead and proceed to your goals, that failure will not stop you.

Creativity and happiness

Happiness favours a creative mind.

You get creative when doing something and nothing. We tend to neglect the activity to do nothing.

Of course when you are working, your creative juices get to work, maybe not always, but possibly sometimes if not most times.

When you got those creative ideas, it was mostly when you were doing nothing; maybe taking a mindless walk, lying on your bed, or not being on twitter (actually doing nothing). To be more creative, give doing nothing a chance, as already you are using creativity when doing that something.

We make decisions in order to get to a point, and then follow with actions to get there. But we want to get to that point in order to fulfil something in us, which gives us happiness. We always strive to do these actions efficiently. But now creativity just pops in and gives us previously unknown ideas on how we can do things. This is a beautiful phenomenon.

Let's give creativity a chance; let's do nothing sometimes, more often.

Make your life easy through prioritizing

How do you get from point A to Z, many put a lot of tedious methods/processes to get there. For instance, a business plan, it's very long and tedious, whereas things change daily. You need it maybe to get finance from a bank, other than that, use the model in this book.

At such a time when you need a business plan for a bank, you can pay an expert to write it for you. Even most venture capitalists or angel investors don't like business plans, they want an understanding of the entrepreneur (happiness and relentlessness), the product, marketing and distribution.

Who says you need to register a company to start a business? It costs money to register a company, are you going to wait till you have the money in order to start a business? Even if you have money for registration, it can be used for something more urgent and progressive. Except if your industry requires only registered business.

Business is about getting to sell, prioritize on what helps you get to SELLING.

Decisions, decisions. Decide! With this money, do I build a website or get business cards? Are most of my customers online or will I meet them in person? Do I use this money to travel and meet potential clients? Or should I rather have a website built and walk to the meetings?

Make decisions that take you closer to achieving the objective (profits). Resources are mostly never enough, swim through anyway.

Reaching happiness through decision

Entrepreneurs are not excluded from unhappiness and dishonesty. Indecisiveness will yield you stress and unhappiness. I'm not saying rush into making decisions, but ultimately you must make a decision. And you improve as you do this.

> *Here is stupid but simple advice on happiness. Say you love roasted chicken, then you get invited to a party and without expecting it they serve roasted chicken which of course makes you happy. But how many parties are you going to walk into that serve roasted chicken?*
>
> *Your decision to live and go to a party got you your favourite dish. So from then you might perhaps decide to go to more parties in the hope of being served roasted chicken. Maybe you might even go as far as calling people up to ask if they will be*

serving roasted chicken at their parties.

However, it could be a lot of work calling people up and going to a lot of parties. The easiest way would be to make or buy your own roasted chicken. What works for you?

You might hate spending your own money, but spending it on roasted chicken will make you happy. Or maybe you are happier not to spend money even on something you love, such as roasted chicken and prefer the trouble of taking chances at parties.

A sacrifice has to be made to get happiness. Even if it's your money, right?

Nonetheless you make decisions to get happiness. You decide which is less troublesome but effective.

So for happiness, you have to make a decision for an anticipated outcome. The sharper the decision, the closer the results!

Example 2. *You want to start a business, you decide to start the business, you go ahead and start it, and you are happy right? Had you decided not to start the business you probably wouldn't have been as happy.*

The challenge maybe is, you are employed and have responsibilities: family to feed, etc. It would be insane to quit right there without knowing what will feed your family. Disclaimer: I'm one of those that quit their jobs without any back up plan in case things didn't come together in time, and they didn't come together in time.

The best thing to do is slaughter your fears in small packages. Start the business while you are employed, run it parallel to your job, just make sure your employee duties are not hampered as result. You have a salary, make use of it and pay other people to do certain things for you. As an entrepreneur you want efficiency, it includes not doing everything yourself.

The main thing is that you decided to do something that makes you happy. At the same time, your salary is still there to cover for those responsibilities you of course care about.

There are many ways to get to a point, decide now that you will seek a solution, happiness will be upon you. Now and then, you will make bad decisions, but you can't get to being an efficient decision maker without having made bad decisions. Practice makes perfect, practice now, not later.

Other relationships

Entrepreneurs are not immune to domestic problems, or whatever problems human beings are subjected to. They can even cause unhappiness to others.

We said efficiency yields happiness. Entrepreneurs need to keep trying out decisions that yield happiness in their personal lives and their loved one's lives.

It's hard keeping this balance. But once family knows you are a decided entrepreneur, they know that you are committed to achieving success in your entrepreneurial venturing, they should help you achieve a balance.

I'm rather unqualified to be going on about a balance between entrepreneurship and family, but I will forever keep trying. Sometimes I get it right, sometimes I don't. I'm happy that I keep trying.

I know entrepreneurship yields me happiness, so does family; choosing one between the two will take some joy away from me. I'm forced to try a balance. I have to guard when the other tries to upset the other. And on that point I have to explore a decision that will put me within happiness.

Communication

I've lost customers because of bad communication, and in most cases it wasn't because I was delaying in finishing their jobs or the jobs thus far were bad.

Communicate with your customers, if you foresee a delay in delivering a product/job; communicate that to the consumer before it becomes a crisis.

Be honest to your consumers of what you can do and what you can't do. Honesty is the basis.

Do this to avoid the crappy feeling of losing shoppers/clients. The repercussions of dishonesty hurt more than those of honesty. Business is about integrity and keeping customers happy, fault happens, but no communication makes it worse. Bad communication signals that you are not to be trusted, which results in losing future business. Unhappy customers tell more people than happy customers, now thanks to social media…

Set clear foundations (memorandum of agreement) with your customers.

It's also crucial to agree on methods and timing of communication with customers. The methods have to be better and convenient for the 2 of you. Using Whatsapp is probably not ideal. You might find yourself in a situation where a client wants to chat about the job all day non stop, which might give an ever changing brief.

Only promise what you can deliver.

Under promise and over deliver! In that way there is no disappointment when the over promises are not delivered. Always over deliver; only finish the required job before the extras (the extras would be the unmentioned over promises).

Decide to be a good communicator.

In closing

With this chapter on happiness, I've tried to share couple of concepts that I use to achieve this which we call happiness. They are maybe not perfect, but I've shared. Sharing is good.

So please share your ways of achieving this happiness here @ tiisetsomalomablog@gmail.com.

Lazy decisions yield nothing but unhappiness. Don't sell your progress short, decide now to do something of fulfilment.

Try and do things right and you will have fewer consequences.

END OF ESSENTIAL BUSINESS COMPONENTS, I.E. THE SHORT BUSINESS MODEL

FAQ

DOES THIS BUSINESS MODEL APPLY ONLY TO PHYSICAL PRODUCT BUSINESSES?

No it doesn't, it applies to all sorts of businesses. A good product/service is marketable, should be marketed in the best way possible, and distributed well and efficiently. That's how profits are realised.

IS THIS BUSINESS MODEL A RULE OF THUMB?

No it's not. I devised this model after I had realised what is important in realising what should be priority in order to profit, in various business industries. It's all about what works for you, leave out or add what you see fit in your particular business, but please do share here tiisetsomalomablog@gmail.com, which I will share with all the other readers of the book.

EBC BUSINESS MODEL CANVAS/INFOGRAPHIC

Donwload for free a copy of the EBC Business Model Canvas/Infographic Checklist here
www.tiisetsomaloma.com/EBCModel.

MOTTOS I LIVE BY

*These are decisions I make every day.

a) Live in the now, meaning work now. Worry thrives on you travelling to the future and past. Working now gets you to your ambitions.

b) Humble thy self to the person you want to become.

c) Don't wait till you have money to show people you love and care for them.

d) All work is fun. No such thing as hard work. Procrastination tells you work is hard.

e) Enjoy listening and explaining to people.

f) Let not small activities keep me off my main objective.

g) Compare self not to others. Think not what people will say about you.

h) Noble ambitions care not if they are laughed at.

i) Courage comes from doing, fear and procrastination cements on not doing now.

j) Picture it a reality. Get your heart into it.

k) Love is the only feeling; forget envy, blame, anger, hate, revenge, etc. With love, you are ever fresh to focus on what matters in helping you to be happy and progress.

l) Fear of what they will say or say, gathers only regret of not having done.

m) The world won't stop on account of those who don't do, but will shape to the tune of those who do.

n) People give up because they stop believing in themselves, and run on believing fearful others.

o) As human beings, we thrive on addictions (coffee, love, gossip, reading, work, hate, etc). Choose your addictions, and wisely.

p) Only those daring with action will get the privilege of knowing failure and success.

q) Money is dependant on time (time is money as they say). Happiness is dependant on NOW. Be happy now.

r) Literacy is awareness on how to move forward as a collective.

s) Yes business is personal, but more on how your personality is able to motivate and sway progress.

t) Dreams must be stronger than pain.

u) The world will reject you many times, but never ever reject you.

v) Rise above self doubt.

w) Let go of your victim mentality and make shit happen for you.

x) Caution: don't lose yourself trying to please or impress others.

Working takes the crap out of procrastination.

www.ingramcontent.com/pod-product-compliance
Lightning Source LLC
Chambersburg PA
CBHW071727170526
45165CB00005B/2191